You're All Right

A Children's Book about Human Similarities

by

Joy Wilt

Illustrated by Ernie Hergenroeder

Educational Products Division
Word, Incorporated
Waco, Texas

Author

JOY WILT is creator and director of Children's Ministries, an organization that provides resources "for people who care about children"—speakers, workshops, demonstrations, consulting services, and training institutes. A certified elementary school teacher, administrator, and early childhood specialist, Joy is also consultant to and professor in the master's degree program in children's ministries for Fuller Theological Seminary. Joy is a graduate of LaVerne College, LaVerne, California (B.A. in Biological Science), and Pacific Oaks College, Pasadena, California (M.A. in Human Development). She is author of two books, *Happily Ever After* and *An Uncomplicated Guide to Becoming a Superparent,* as well as the popular *Can-Make-And-Do Books.* Joy's commitment "never to forget what it feels like to be a child" permeates the many innovative programs she has developed and her work as lecturer, consultant, writer, and—not least—mother of two children, Christopher and Lisa.

Artist

ERNIE HERGENROEDER is owner and operator of Hergie & Associates (an advertising agency and graphics production house). His desire to draw came at the early age of three, and all through high school he achieved top honors in art. In 1961 he joined the United States Air Force, and became the Wing Commander's personal illustrator. From 1965 to 1975 he owned and operated a successful sign company in Sonora, California. In 1975 he sold his business in order to devote his full attention to drawing cartoons. Ernie, his wife Faith, and their four children Lynn, Kathy, Stephen, and Beth now reside in San Jose, California.

You're All Right

Contents

Introduction

<u>You're All Right</u> is one of a series of books. The complete set is called *Ready-Set-Grow!*

<u>You're All Right</u> deals with human similarities, and can be used by itself or as part of a program that utilizes all of the *Ready-Set-Grow!* books.

<u>You're All Right</u> is specifically designed for children four to eight years of age. A child can either read the book or have it read to him or her. This can be done at home, church, or school.

<u>You're All Right</u> is designed to involve the child in the concepts that are being taught. This is done by simply and carefully explaining each concept and then asking questions that invite a response from the child. It is hoped that by answering the questions the child will personalize the concept and, thus, integrate it into his or her thinking.

A lot has been written about the importance of each child having a positive self-concept, but very little has been said about how a positive self-concept can be developed. If children are to think well of themselves, they must realize and accept the fact that they are human beings — persons.

Once they have grasped this concept, they can begin to understand that because they are persons, they share similarities with other people and that the similarities they share are "all right"!

This can be redeeming for children because there are many things about a child's body that embarrasses him or her and, thus, hinders him or her from having a positive attitude. A child can find comfort in the fact that the bodily functions that often embarrass him or her are also experienced by other human beings.

It is also affirming for a child to know that just as he or she has accidents, makes wrong choices, and makes mistakes, so do other people. This is the same with so-called negative feelings. Everyone has them. They are a real part of every person. A child needs to know that feelings, in and of themselves, are neither good nor bad. It's how one handles one's feelings, or what one does as a result of feelings, that makes a good or bad situation.

Children, for obvious psychological and emotional reasons, need to be allowed to express their negative feelings. Our responsibility is to help them learn to express their feelings in acceptable ways. There is right and wrong behavior, but value judgments on the rightness or wrongness of specific behavior lie outside the scope of this book. Behavioral standards, while necessary to the moral growth of children, must first find the fertile ground of a positive self-concept before they can be effectively internalized. You're All Right seeks to prepare a child for making these standards his or her own.

You're All Right has a specific goal: building a positive self-concept within a child by affirming his or her membership in the human family. You're All Right does this first by teaching a child that he or she is similar to other human beings and that the similarities he or she has in common with others are normal. Second, You're All Right teaches a child that when God created him or her, God did not make any mistakes. Everything God does has a purpose and fits into a total plan. Being a person is a part of God's plan for every human being. Children who grow up believing and accepting this will be equipped to live healthy, exciting lives.

You are "all right."

Do you know what it means to be "all right"?

If you do not know what it means to be
all right, that's OK because . . .

this book will tell you all about it.

CHAPTER 1

You Are a Person

I AM PROUD TO BE A PERSON.

The dictionary says that . . .

a person is a man, woman, or child.

Because you are a child, you are a person.
When you grow up and become a man or a woman,
you will still be a person.

Each one of us is a person.

What does it mean to be a person?

CHAPTER 2

A Person Has a Body

In many ways every person's body is like that of every other person.

How is that true?

Every person has . . .

a head

and a body.

Every person has . . .

arms, hands, and fingers

and legs, feet, and toes.

Every person has . . .

eyes to see with and ears to hear with

and skin to feel with.

31

Every person has . . .

a nose to smell with

and a mouth to taste with.

In order to stay alive every person must . . .

move his or her body

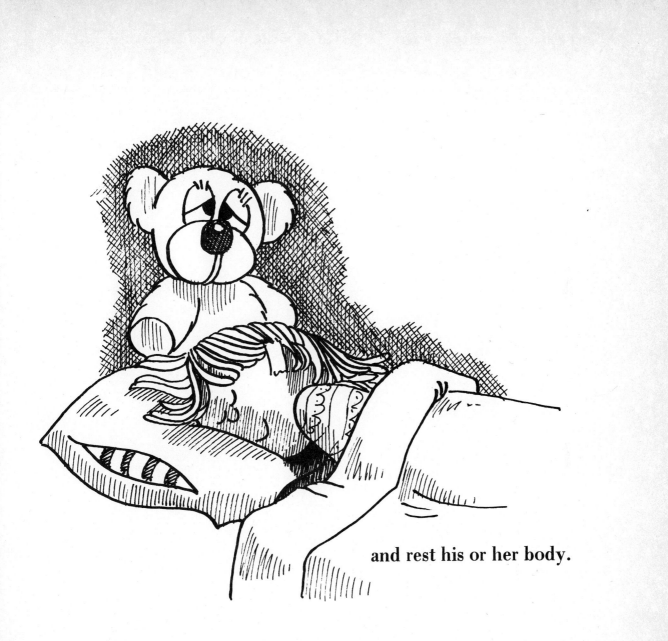

and rest his or her body.

In order to stay alive every person must . . .

eat and drink

and breathe air.

In order to stay alive every person must . . .

eliminate waste from his or her body (go to the bathroom).

Many people feel embarrassed about . . .

going to the bathroom.

What was your reaction to the pictures on the four pages before this one?

Did you giggle?
Did you feel embarrassed?

How did you feel?

Many people feel embarrassed about . . .

vomiting (throwing up) when they are sick.

45

Many people feel embarrassed about . . .

sneezing,

hiccupping,

passing gas, and burping.

Many people feel embarrassed about . . .

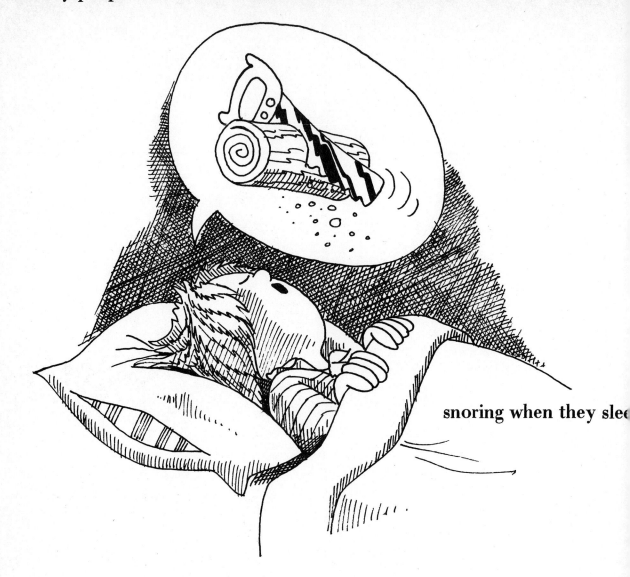

snoring when they slee

and their stomachs growling

(making rumbling sounds)

when they are hungry.

Are you embarrassed about . . .

Going to the bathroom?
Vomiting (throwing up)?
Hiccupping?
Sneezing?
Burping?
Passing gas?
Snoring when you sleep?

Your stomach growling

(making rumbling sounds)

when you are hungry?

You don't need to be embarrassed or feel bad about doing these things when you have to, because every person sometimes does them. They are things that a person's body does to keep the person alive, well, and comfortable.

And because your body was created by God . . .

You can be proud of your body.

Besides having bodies that are, in many ways, alike . . .

What does it mean to be a person?

CHAPTER 3

Sometimes a Person Has Unhappy Feelings

Every person, at some time, feels . . .

angry (mad

and guilty (like he or she has done something wrong).

Every person, at some time, feels . . .

grief (sadness)

and lonely (all alone).

Every person, at some time, feels . . .

humiliated (embarrassed, put down),

rejected (not accepted by others),

and frightened (scared).

Every person, at some time, feels . . .

anxious (nervous).

Every person, at some time, feels . . .

frustrated (discouraged)

and defeated (beaten).

Do you ever feel . . .

Mad (angry)?

Guilty (like you did something wrong)?

Grief (sadness)?

Lonely (all alone)?

Humiliated (embarrassed, put down)?

Rejected (not accepted by others)?

Frightened (scared)?

Anxious (nervous)?

Frustrated (discouraged)?

Defeated (beaten)?

You don't need to be embarrassed or feel bad about feeling these feelings because every person feels them.

You are a person, and at some time or another you will feel all kinds of feelings just as every other person does.

You are a person with feelings, and that is something you can be proud of because God created you with feelings.

What does it mean to be a person?

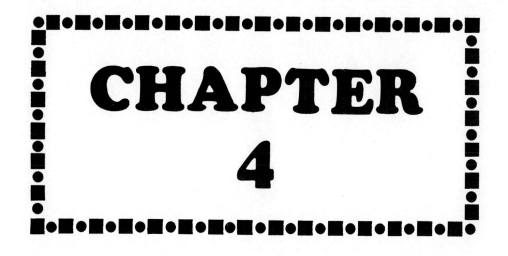

CHAPTER 4

Sometimes a Person Has Accidents

Besides feeling all kinds of feelings . . .

Every person, no matter who he or she is,
sometimes has accidents like . . .

spilling things

or breaking things.

Every person, no matter who he or she is, sometimes has accidents like . . .

tripping over things

or bumping into things.

Do you have accidents like . . .

Spilling things?
Breaking things?
Tripping over things?
Bumping into things?

You don't need to be embarrassed or feel bad about the fact that you have accidents. Every person sometimes has accidents.

God created you a person, and because you are, you will sometimes have accidents just as every other person does.

It is true that no person wants to have an accident, and so every person tries to be careful so that he or she won't have accidents. But even so . . .

Every person has accidents.

What does it mean to be a person?

CHAPTER 5

Sometimes a Person Makes Wrong Choices

Besides having accidents . . .

Every person, no matter who he or she is,
sometimes makes wrong choices like . . .

YUCK!
I THOUGHT BANAN
LICORICE ICE CREA
WOULD TASTE
GOOD.

choosing the wrong things to ea

or choosing the wrong things to wear.

Every person, no matter who he or she is, sometimes makes wrong choices like . . .

choosing the wrong people to be with

or choosing the wrong things to do.

Do you make wrong choices like . . .

Choosing the wrong things to eat?

Choosing the wrong things to wear?

Choosing the wrong people to be with?

Choosing the wrong things to do?

You don't need to be embarrassed or feel bad about the fact that you make wrong choices. Every person sometimes makes wrong choices.

God created you a person, and because you are, you will sometimes make wrong choices just as every other person does.

It is true that after a person makes a wrong choice, he or she usually learns to think carefully before making another choice. But even so . . .

Every person makes wrong choices.

What does it mean to be a person?

CHAPTER 6

Sometimes a Person Makes Mistakes

Besides making wrong choices . . .

Every person, no matter who he or she is,
sometimes makes mistakes . . .

while talking

and while reading.

Every person, no matter who he or she is,
sometimes makes mistakes . . .

while spelling

and while writing.

Every person, no matter who he or she is, sometimes makes mistakes . . .

while doing arithmetic

and while doing experiments.

Every person, no matter who he or she is,

sometimes makes mistakes . . .

while making things

and while singing, or playing a musical instrument.

Every person, no matter who he or she is, sometimes makes mistakes . . .

while playing games

and while performing.

Do you make mistakes . . .

While talking?
While reading?
While spelling?
While writing?
While doing arithmetic?
While doing experiments?
While making things?
While singing, or playing a musical instrument?
While playing games?
While performing?

You don't need to be embarrassed or feel bad about the fact that you make mistakes. Every person sometimes makes mistakes.

God created you a person, and because you are, you will sometimes make mistakes just as every other person does.

It is true that no one wants to make mistakes, and so every person tries to be careful so that he or she won't make any. But even so . . .

Every person makes mistakes.

So what does it mean to be "all right"?

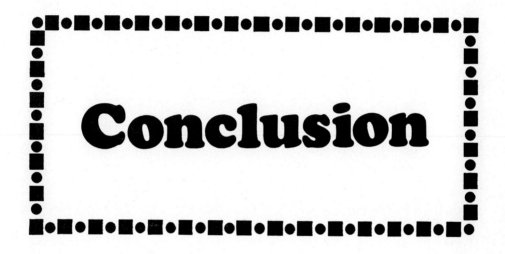

God created you a person, and
because you are one . . .

You have a body that does what seems to be strange things.
You feel all kinds of feelings.
Sometimes you have accidents.
Sometimes you make wrong choices.
Sometimes you make mistakes.

And . . .